SLAG

AIMEE NOEL
SLAG

Poems

Sheila-Na-Gig Editions

Cover design: KaiserDicken
Cover top photo: Getty Images/iStock Photo
Cover bottom photo: Craig Dicken
Author photo: Carrie Scarff

ISBN: 9781962405409
Library of Congress Control Number: 2025944604

Sheila-Na-Gig Editions
Russell, KY
Hayley Mitchell Haugen, Editor
www.sheilanagigblog.com

Acknowledgments

Thank you to the editors of the following journals and anthologies in which these poems originally appeared:

Belt: A Dayton Anthology: "All Together Now"

Common Threads: "Mill Days"

Eclipsing the Dark Anthology: "Chasing the Moon" (as "Future Eclipses")

Ecotone: "Bless the Water"

Forklift, Ohio: "Returning to Work after the Women's March"

Great Lakes Review: "Baking Uranium," "Calculating Exposure," "Inverted Water"

Hanging Loose: "Bucha, Ukraine," "The Child and the Quicksilver," "Hereditary Border"

Ilanot Review: "Bedtime," "Luxury of Snow"

Michigan Quarterly Review: "Hierarchy of Fish"

Mock Turtle Zine: "Going Home Again"

Nuclear Impact Anthology: "Faster Than Math" (as "A Death Faster than Math")

Pittsburgh Poetry Journal: "Language is the Only Homeland"

Provincetown Arts: "Understanding Gear Ratios"

Witness: "Delayed Internment"

for Carrie and the echoes of Gambier

Contents

I

The Child and the Quicksilver   15
Understanding Gear Ratios   16
How to Get to the Town Park All by Yourself   17
Bedtime   18
Danger Signs   19
Chasing the Moon   20
The Shores of Anywhere   21
Hierarchy of Fish   22
Bless the Water   23
Apologies to a Hometown   24
Slag   25

II

Earth Day   29
Instead of lockers   30
dust   31
Mill Days   32
After Swing Shift   33
The Day I Moved Up   34
Rebuttal   35
Baking Uranium   36
Calculating Exposure   37
Rosie No More   39
Butcher, Baker, Uranium Maker   41
Faster Than Math   42
Subpono   44
Lake Erie: Clean Fill Wanted   45
The son casts his own line   46
Delayed Internment   47
dust   48

III

Circe Mulling Wine   51
Sales Tips   52
To Scarborough Fair   53
Attendance   54
I think as I watch you breathe   56
Party of One   57
Unnamed Woman   58
Urban Spring   59
Returning to Work After the Women's March   60
Bucha, Ukraine   61
All Together Now   62
Witness   64
Forgive Us Our Trespasses   66

IV

Hereditary Border   69
How Wonderful to Love   70
Final Exam   71
Body of Work   72
Language is the only homeland   74
St. Michael Taxiarchi's Shrine   75
Going Home Again   76
Luxury of Snow   77
Wherever You Go   78
Inverted Water   80

Notes   83

Slag /slæg/ · *n*. waste material
formed by oxidation at the surface of
molten metals; *slang*. an offensive term
for a woman used to insinuate she is lewd
or promiscuous

It is a dangerous thing to forget
the climate of your birthplace

—from Judith Ortiz Cofer's *El Ovido*

I

The Child and the Quicksilver

When the streetlight breaks, I coax its mercury
    into a Dixie cup to paint myself silver. Nightly
        I sluice quicksilver from palm to palm watching
            my life line drown under its weight. Every time
                I pour the liquid mirror back into the cup, there is less
            of me reflected. When only a bead remains, I swirl it
        around the bottom, as if quickening minutes on a clock,
    then pool it in my navel to prove I am metal-fed. *Listen*, I say,
I can float steel on my surface. Look at my coat of shine.

Understanding Gear Ratios

Because everything my father valued was shiny, I tried
to wrap myself in chrome or fire myself crucible-hot,

pour slag from my throat until he believed I was
tempered steel and a son. After school I snapped

tools into his open palm like a surgical assistant
while he resuscitated junkyard cars. Bedtime

lullabies of socket sizes and spark plug gappings
seeped from my brain like spent oil into a drip pan.

Fractions and meters and gear ratios would not remain
in my mind of words: 2:1 spinning in the opposite direction.

How to Get to the Town Park All by Yourself

You want to walk the whole way barefoot,
but at the door you can already smell
the oil drizzled to keep the dust down—
like someone gutted a transmission in the road.

So you put shoes on, follow those lazy loops
to the "T" at the mulberry tree.

You can go left, but you'll dead-end
at Ann's yellow house. She knows your mom
and will let you cut through if her husband
isn't dressed in women's clothes right then.

Your mom wonders
if Ann's still happy
she married Mark
and if she feels cheated on—
but a different kind of cheating.

You wonder
what his leg hair feels like
caught under pantyhose.

It will be a long time
before anyone wonders
how Mark feels.

He has boxes and boxes
of limestone fossils he found
at the beach and can tell you
about each life trapped inside.

Bedtime

Fish-fry fed, my dad led me out the back of Elmer's Grill,
        bedtime,
and warned not to unlock our truck for anyone. I didn't

know enough to care about my clothes as I
        camouflaged
myself deep behind the seats, watching headlights leave

for homes where children slept in a bed. I
        clutched
keys to places I'd never been, mysterious as tackle box

lures. Too tired to arrange a bed from the fan belts,
        work shirts,
and coils of hoses, I surrendered

in whichever direction I fell, onto a
        mattress
of coveralls smelling of my dad's hamper.

I never remember falling asleep, so I was always
        startled
by the one-knuckled knock on the window.

My body bent over the front seats, I would
        stretch
to pull the door handle open. Closing time.

Danger Signs

The trick, Dad said, was tying a red flag
to the end. Whatever barely-dented

fender or odd length of rebar
we scavenged could hang itself

over the hood of the car behind us
as long as a scrap of flannel marked

the danger. Like most rules he bent
to his convenience, I never checked

its validity, wanting to believe
that if I signaled a warning,

life would give me a wide berth
and I'd return the favor. Vigilant,

I'd watch the blanket of crimson
baseball caps before a podium,

a ruby toggle in the ballot box,
a smoky flash in the sky before each side

fights to be most right. Just hint enough
to square my shoulders or stay away.

Chasing the Moon

I was seven when I discovered the moon
like a river rock, smooth and floating
in the pin-holed heaven. So taken was I

with its halo, I walked the length of my drive
keeping a side-eye on the orb as if only my vision
pinned the spectacle to the sky. How far,

I wondered, could I wander with the moon
over my shoulder like a celestial souvenir
at the end of my string. There, too, it was

in the backyard, blue light pooled
across three lawns and the scrabbly hedges
separating each. I called to Laura, a yard away,

swimming in the light. The moon
shone on us just the same. Its face fixed
by our wonder. I ran and she ran

to the front to test the lunar staying power.
I kicked a rocky wake in sneakers so thin
my soles ground the gravel peaks beneath my feet.

We hollered our sightings like scientists conducting
the most special of experiments: our place in space.
We did not yet know the moon was a shape-shifter

slicing off parts of itself so no one could find it cloaked
behind its own dark, having pulled covers over its shine,
refusing to face the night. Decades later I learned

the moon did not have Laura's best interest at heart.
Man, having already landed on the pristine surface,
would leave his mark with no wind enough to erase it.

The Shores of Everywhere

For decades money pumped toxins into clean bodies
of water then walked away. This water swallowed the spoils
as if its job were to keep the secrets of men. Waves wore

sun-glinted jewels on the surface as a distraction, and we did
our part. We accepted blame for our melancholy and stillbirths
and for land which no longer sustained life. We slid our feet

along Lake Erie's bottom, barely creating a ripple, while poison
made its way up the food chain. A settling occurred, and, as long
as undisturbed, the world could forget the threat was there.

This is not news to you. Your eyes are on a gathering storm
that will churn layers of hubris to the surface, with clouds
ready to set loose rains until a swift enough current
washes away any trace of power protecting itself.

Hierarchy of Fish

When there is nothing
left to eat, carp walk
across fetid mats of algae

and lay themselves
like silver loaves
along the shore.

Fattened on slag,
mud vein heavy
with metal, they

return to our plates,
replete with floating bones,
what we have given.

Bless the Water

Bless the water so abundant in my youth,
absent of mercury or algae blooms
or zebra mussels' future invasion.

Bless my ignorance of the same.

Bless the ways in which this lake
absorbed a community's abuse.

Bless my ignorance of the same.

Bless the frothy-fingered waves
that welcomed me at my worst.

Bless the sand that scrubbed this city's
rust from my skin until I was new enough
to move through a different space,
far from my water-born days.

Bless the luxury of walking
on thin ice with abandon,
the belief that its crazed surface
would always hold me
like a martyr or a mother.

Bless my ignorance of the same.

Apologies to a Hometown

Forgive me, Buffalo. I consumed you.
Ate your chicken wing wisdom

and tossed the bones, mounding
like matchsticks, into wooden bowls,

devoured Lenten fish as if its white flakes
were the wafered body of Christ.

Drank your Niagara World Wonder
with I-beam pride then stole away

into a four-year night. I waved goodbye
to gatehouse ghosts and you didn't

put up a fight. The whole city
laid out on ice, I lined my pockets

with the guilt of good judgment
and left you hiding your hurt

under dingy skirts of snow. Who knew
this love affair would be distant?

That my lake-effect temper would storm
in a cornfield, whispering stalks no match

for waves to lull me back into my skin.
I build steel dust scarecrows to honor people

who bent their backs building the bridge
across which I left you, a jilted lover.

Slag

I.

Imagine giant cauldrons
slung along the shoreline
on rails, rocking on swivels
as the train stops. The vats
tipped like teacups and
molten slag slides down
the bank. Rivers alongside
eddy and cool to red while
an orange stream tracks
its own thermal path straight
to the lake. Great explosions
plume rust-colored smoke
as water and waste exchange
energy and boil everything
in its wake. The by-product
sinks, becomes blue, cracks itself
like glass, tumbles over sand until
edges disappear. It emerges a gem,
a smooth memory a child finds
along the shore and rubs absently
with a thumb, an industrial fairy tale.

II.

Blue to draw your eye from the horizon
Blue you'd swear was a turquoise
Blue like this lake never was
Blue like the sky cracked open
Blue like eyes you can't stop listening to
Blue like the Monet at a gallery you've yet to see
that will make you weep and walk out of this town

II

Earth Day

When I say *earth*, I mean grit
between teeth of workers who shovel
coal into open hearth furnaces

bodies bent by heavy metals
and the weight of limited options

rust flaking from corroded locks
on gates where whistles blew
for the barstool's second shift

grime wiped from wash drums
after a load of work clothes

soot smearing itself inside
lungs where breath should be

silt sifted through resignation
settling into layers on the windshield so fine
you'd swear your vision was not impaired

Instead of lockers

steel pails with hooks
welded to the sides,
part bait bucket, part lure,
swing at the ends of cables
from a ceiling too high to see.

These lines, cast to numbered poles,
lock for safe-keeping. Steel men
begin and end in this *welfare room*,
securing their keys and pride up high.

On hooks they hang whole selves,
shells of street clothing: denim,
cotton, rubber-soled shoes.
Single-ply tinder hangs like effigies
of their street beings for ten hours.

Suspended in this open-air locker,
two-hundred husks collect
the thrum and churn,
heat and ash of the plant.

When men lower chains
to reclaim uniforms
of dad and spouse,
clouds secret themselves
in the clothing's folds
for the journey home
to plume anew.

dust

that settled in coffee

filtered past nose hairs

clambered up laces

stowed away in tool bags

smoothed in grooves of boot tread

coated insides of wedding bands

clung to crib sheets

hung out to dry

in a mill town

did not exist

Mill Days

All singed flesh smells the same, metallic
stab in your nose setting teeth to ache,

whether the meal cooling at home
includes lentils or borscht or Bolognese.

The stink of burning slag coats a city,
blows across every bridge until there's nothing

left to do but shoot a president,
name a street where women

fly white curtains, scrub
wash tubs of orange dust.

The canary in steel mill generations:
stronger, dead younger, fed on roots.

Beet-red pocks, burnt eyes through
hollow sockets. Cotton, a paper flower

in a conflagration. Someone's uncle,
anthracite and alloy for lunch, prays.

Bellows blow galvanized prayers,
blistering the oxygen into English.

After Swing Shift

We go to Elmer's [or Mickey's or The
Grill] on the corner of Family and Mill.
We cash paychecks for perch [or wings
or dogs and kraut] that comes on plates
pinky-finger thick, ringed with the blue
of steel tempered at 580 degrees. We
throw in money for the football pool
[or picnic or Phil's family] and fold the
rest into weathered wallets. We drink our
Stroh's [or Genny or Schlitz] slow so
that we have something to show come
morning. And Larry [or Eric or Frank]
serves beer on corrugated coasters cut
from boxes of pickles [or pretzels or
pickled eggs]. Our hands form a perfect
curl from gripping a sledge [or shaft or
glass] for hours. The dust in our knuckles
oxidizes to rust, maps the work of the
open hearth [or roller mill or furnace].
The jukebox plays The Stones [or
Hendrix or nothing] as we talk about
bowling [or bait or whether Phil's wife
will move after the funeral]. Or we argue
about the same. And we leave at 2:00 [or
5:00 or stay until 7:00 and tell our wives
we worked a double].

Moving Up Day

—for Robert Robinson (Bethlehem Steel, 1951-1996)

Every year, for thirty years,
hands up, and they shot him
through in two dimensions same

as he walked the floor: faceless, flat.
Except this year the company doctor,
says pointing to a shadow

on the picture-film, he says *TB* and
the foreman hands Bobby a broom.
Black man's promotion, TB.

So they move him from furnace to production,
and he waits for the cough to come. He drums up
dust plumes in two-feet paths and pushes

that flurry through to the end of the planks.
He scrapes scale and pushes dust and waits
to see his lungs, pulpy and bloody, in a tissued hand.

Nineteen pills, ten-hour shifts, two-foot paths.
Daily. And the dust, it don't move but falls through
the planks, coating electricians and other rats

like a cake waiting to be lit. TB is trumped
by a plateful of perch and a bone that sticks
in his throat. Hospital doctor says his pain

ain't the bone, ain't a disease, ain't being
stooped over a broom, but a tumor in his back,
three pounds now, and would he like to be rid of it?

Rebuttal

—after Deacon Ollie Allen

They didn't have T.B.

It was the lung

eaten up

with steel particles.

Baking Uranium, 1942

Your grandma, she was the best cook, not sweets
but metal. Could roll those sheets so thin.
      Ingredients brought by the trainful.
      No recipe necessary,
      she could dash
           and smidge
                and pinch her way
to perfection. Could stretch a recipe, too.

Make it last.

They served her goods to foreign men
      who were never heard from again.

And what of the surplus, you say?

The government, radiating happiness,
ignored the extra going home
with your grandma.

She had a shaker of it up her sleeve.
Her bouffant was a cloud of it.

On weekends she'd
shimmy her skirt
and dazzle the men

until they were all wasted
on her secret ingredient.

Even when the recipe
made her lungs into

      paperweights,

she would not reveal the magic.
Swore she did not know.

Calculating Exposure

—taken from interviews with steelworkers
Joe Ed Lawrence and Ted Priester

In those days we took a test
for a better mill job an' the reason
that was so hard—
they had things like algebra
that you take for granted now.

Set parameters using the dose coefficients for inhalation:
einh(50) for 1 μm AMAD [Sv/Bq]

It was a mechanical test, could you read a rule,
an' then they would have the numbers
like 5/16, 7/16, 3/8 on there,
they have them mixed up.

For ingestion: eing(50)[Sv/Bq]

They say put them in order,
which is the lowest up
to the highest, quarter inch, an eighth,
an' you did that.

For external exposure: [Sv/h per Bq/cm^3]

Then they asked you about if the gear is turning
to the right clockwise an' this shaft
is turning to the left or which way—
if it turned counterclockwise,
which way would the shaft turn,
an' you had to answer it,
you had to figure it out whichever way.

The solubility class can be selected
according to the chemical form of the uranium:
F: UF_6, UO_2F_2, $UO_2(NO_3)_2$ ($f_1 = 0.02$)
M: UO_3, UF_4, UCl_4 ($f_1 = 0.02$)
S: UO_2, U_3O_8 ($f_1 = 0.002$)

They asked you about bearings an' about seals,
what kind of—they have different kinds
of seals, leather seals, maybe plastic—
I don't know about the plastic at the time,
but anyway, a lot of mechanical questions
an' then math

Occupational Annual Limits on Intake (ALI's) for Inhalation
$U_{natural}$ (soluble): 1 µCi (= 37000 Bq, equiv. to 1.5 g)
$U_{natural}$ (insoluble): 0.05 µCi (= 1850 Bq, equiv. to 74 mg)

You had to do math, add an' subtract,
multiply an' divide an' fractions an'
changing fractions to decimal, decimal
to fractions. You had to do that also.
So it was a pretty tough test.

Rosie No More

—for the women of steel

Rosie with her ruby lips
shining off the camera flash,
her hair wrapped like a gift.

> *We scrub the female from our faces.*
> *In the winter we're issued flannel and*
> *in the summer the same, insulated*
> *like live wires among men*
> *who claim our bodies*
> *distract from production*

Rosie, beloved for her sacrifice,
patriotic poster child:
piercing metal flesh with rivets.

> *We are passed over for promotions.*
> *We train each new recruit. Foremen*
> *throw our tools into the furnace*
> *when we're not looking. Or when we are.*

Her sweetheart home, Rosie about-faces
to the kitchen, a ric rac apron tied around
her waist, her neck smelling of vanilla.

> *We marry our machines. Men propose*
> *to tie us and screw us if we can't*
> *pull our weight. We work*
> *swing shift, night shift, double shifts.*

Rosie pushes a baby-buggy mid-day;
the hood shades sun and dust. The child
sleeps to the metronome of heels on sidewalk.

We are declared unfit mothers. We lose
custody. Best we can hope for is to be
"one of the guys," to hand over our
womanhood and earn, come retirement,
nestled on a satin pillow, our own brass balls.

Butcher, Baker, Uranium Maker

Pass your kidney, your liver, your lungs across
the stainless counter so he can slap them

on the scale. Pray the digits rise this time
to meet the maker's mile, the actuary's

unknowable, incalculable, unreachable
number to prove your end had metal

beginnings. Stare at your kidney, your liver,
your lungs to see if they have gained

the weight of evidence for your serial
wheezing, bent-over stabs, sooty coughs.

He's the mill's man. You're not convinced
his sleight of hand didn't lop off a slab

on the way to the scale, feeding feral cats
at his feet. Watch the number stall

nowhere near the range for reparations.
He folds your kidney, your liver, your lungs

into glossy wax wrap, slides the pillowed parcel across
the counter, dismisses you with a sidewise wave, barks, *Next!*

Faster Than Math

Steel men are dying, see,
faster than widows can figure
the equations. A colon closed
down + a rectum sewn shut,

equals

they carry their life's waste
outside of their bodies
in clear plastic bags for all
to see, not making it to meetings
- tallying enough numbers

equals

an absence of legs to move them
there. But the miracle of math
will weigh each limb's worth:
heavy metal + heated
elements + Cold War

equals

if their breathing can be sub-
contracted a few more years
until their pension kicks in; Dying
at graphing calculator rates, men
spike thirty years after the last (alleged)
uranium billet + rolled onto the train
        -     (conductor now dead)

equals

lungs to hold six more pounds
before the dosage will be enough
to honor their lives. Calculations
taken from soil, not people and
the polyps are processing +
processing + processing

equals

they'd like to provide you with
more information but those papers
were ≥ burnt paper flakes filtered
through hairs of the janitor's broom.
He'd push the files back but

equals

he's too dead for that.

Subpono

—after Mohja Kahf

Should a worker's body be unrecoverable following an accident,
the company would sometimes present a 140 lb slab of steel or
iron to the family so that they may have something to bury.
—Youngstown Historical Center of Labor & Industry

I love the broken body
and the smooth slab steel
I love the worker who goes
through the gates to break
and the family who buries
the bones or who cannot
I have been the worker who
strides easily through the gate
and the unrecoverable one
whose flesh is never found
I have been the family lowering bones
and the family with a slab of steel
like an anvil across which life is shaped
the percussive strikes on that anvil
and the resonance just after
I am the body and the steel and the strike

Lake Erie: Clean Fill Wanted

Water closes over molten slag 'til poisons never show.
We've ground by-product into sand you can't tell
from real land, and there's millions in tax credits to say so.

We'll just fill a small part—eighty acres is actually low.
With at least that to spare, we just want our share
and have permits from your town council that say so.

There's still perch a-plenty; we monitor their ebb and flow.
It's not shown, to date, that the fish from this lake are not safe
and there's local grocers and butchers who say so.

The laws tie our hands; our waste needs to go.
We've got orders to fill and competition to kill
& you have twenty-thousand jobs that say so.

The son casts his own line

having watched the father this whole summer:
a side-arm sling with bait hurling
the length of its tether. The son snaps

the release catch closed and waits
with the patience of an apprentice to see
what this great lake will bring. By six,

their stringer full, the son hoists a haul
the length of his body, a garland of fish,
folding onto themselves: all striped scales,

glistening yellow underbellies. Waterlines
wave a web across his face as a Polaroid
churns out the next generation's provider

beaming under the weight of dinner. The son holds
the line a bit from his body like the father taught him.
The father won't scare him off with praise or a pat

on the back because his crossing
this divide is more regal than that, and
you don't tell a prince what he already knows.

Delayed Internment

It's April before we can bury our dead.
The ground refuses our immediate grief,
so we preserve it like summer perch

and guard our memories against premature thaw.
This city is harsh like that, makes you sit
with your ghosts. Men frozen in chambray,

weave fraying white at the blue collar,
take shifts on barstools waiting for the world
to tilt back their way. The factory stacks its outline:

an amusement park skeleton for the whole city to ride.
Yous punch your ticket and yous take your chances.
Only the snowplow sparks now, scraping pavement

as it passes men used to swinging hammers and handles
of metal lunch pails. They wait for blast furnaces to return
womb-warm and for the earth to yield to their shovel again.

dust

            wisped by brooms,

                    stirred to the swirl
                    of summer lake-effect snow or

        shed
                              in great scrapes

          of shovel tips,

                      inches thick, from

the heavyweights

        of hell,

        burying men's mettle

                  did not exist

III

Circe Mulling Wine

—by artist Gioacchino Assereto, c. 1630

Stirring, stirring, stirring as women always are,

Circe grips the glowing poker in the silver tureen of wine

deftly, more like a baton, between thumb and forefinger.

Her left hand pauses aloft as if holding an orchestra

at rest. A ruby draws the gaze to the center of her belt,

wide as it is golden, part armor, part trophy. Beside her,

open-mouthed in an Olympic cheer, a winged nymph

forms the handle of an urn, urging the goddess in her work.

Together they perfect the potion to turn men into pigs.

Plotting, plotting, plotting as women always are. *Accelerando.*

Sales Tips

—All text taken from *Direct Replies to Customers' Excuses (Second Edition)*, a pamphlet published for door-to door salesmen, The Fuller Brush Company c. 1930

Do not high pressure your prospect
or she will be afraid of you.

Agree with her.
Ask a question.
Make suggestions.

Never lose your temper. Remember
the customer doesn't understand.

When a customer offers excuses
or an objection, she is telling you
she is half-sold. The customer has
merely indicated her interest
in a negative way.

Say: *That's what many ladies tell me.*

Say: *I am sure your husband will compliment you on your good
judgment.*

Say: *I'm just the man you're looking for. I'm the service man.*
Say: *I will just take a moment to leave your new gift and be on my way.*
Say: *You don't mind if I step in a moment while I give you the service
you're entitled to?*
Say: *It is my duty to give you your new gift. I will step in a moment.*
Say: *I'll just step in and you can make your choice.*
Say: *I'll step right in and give you another.*

Emphasize satisfaction
and objections become insignificant.

Emphasize service
and resistance melts.

To Scarborough Fair

Are you going to Scarborough Fair?
Parsley, sage, rosemary, and thyme
Remember me to one who lives there
She once was a true love of mine
                    —"Scarborough Fair" Simon & Garfunkel

Taken against my will, I was
tasked with the impossible.

Simon and Garfunkel sang
their witness. A shirt without seams

or needlework smothered my back, pressed
my chest into the bed, my dry well

ploughed between salt water and
semen by a ram's horn. Sheets

bore the blossom while my mind
had already run from me to gather:

Parsley for bitterness.
Sage for healing.
Rosemary for remembrance.
Thyme for courage.
Thyme for courage.

Attendance

It's October and I don't know
the girls' names. I know

for another year or so I can safely call
       Hailey or *Megan* or *Brittney*

and there'll be one of those. Their appearance
like a prescription for deflecting attention.
       Hayley or *Meghan* or *Brittany*

smooths her hair
slick as a magazine page,
paint-by-number lowlights,
with this year's accessory:
three pearls
on a brown, braided thread,
nestled in the oyster of her neck.
Jeans ripped just so.

I move them like human buoys
among the reefs of boys.
       Hailee, and *Meagan*, and *Britney*,

though buffeted by waves of conversation
between Keeton and Chase,

remain silent. At fourteen, they have already learned

to laugh at the boy's jokes. Not too long.
Not too loud. I hand them papers
to pass out—though Blake is already roaming.
And when Gabe needs a pencil or gum or homework,

the girls give on demand. We have taught them
to come prepared. They open their flowered
pouches and give up the goods.

To begin the lesson, I have taught them,
we all wait on the boys.

I think as I watch you breathe

of fish, fed on steel,

that swim in me. Heavy

with the weight of grieving,

they sank into my hands.

I carried them home,

arranged them in a vase,

watched their choral gasping.

Party of One

I want to have my mind around the brokenness. To see it coming way off, like a pre-dawn approach of the lone rider in a Western. Sun back-lit, the face of my pain is unknown, but I'll be damned if I am taken unawares. And, if I'm lucky, I'll have a full bucket of popcorn planted on my hip and I've already gone to the bathroom because I want all my energy for the breaking. Poe had it right all along: we have a sick sense of self-loathing. Why else would White Castle be open after 11:00 pm? Why would yoga pants sparkle with embellishments if they weren't going to be our all-the-time pants? I can pretend I've exercised recently, and you can pretend to believe it. More likely I've gotten couch-comfortable to watch my anguish riding full gallop. Horse's hooves: four dusty tornadoes. Preparing, I'll spool my heart strings like Rapunzel's hair, denying access to any thick-voiced scamp who thinks he'll save me. No way. This is my demise, and I'm watching it in HD. The sun sinks, I tune my ear to the stirrup-slapping of my targeted heart, but the rider has made little progress, so I settle in, preening. Poe knew that we love to pick at our own scabs to repeat the bleeding, to continue scraping our nails at the crusty edge long past our ability to see under the blood. We drive by houses where the location of every bed in every room is embedded into our back muscles and look for cars we don't recognize. We have a gift of self-infliction which is why, with my popcorn clouds down to the crumbles, The Cure is on repeat, lyrics not words so much as settings, and I remember the blanket's smell, grabbed from the love seat to cover handsex during the movie where a heart-break rider is following a scent. I lean toward the screen and spy his chap-ladden thighs. I face the dust storm that will scratch my heart opaque. This time I will have seen it coming and will be more beautiful because broken.

Unnamed Woman

Oh, for me to be the "X" in a poem.
To be so feared or loved or both,

to color a memory with layers of paint
until I can't be peeled back.

ABCDEFGHInsert myself in an alphabetJKLMNOPQRSTUVW

and reappear as "X" in verse where my force is
too potent to print

as if the collateral damage of dropping
my identity into the poem would scatter
any other words. Only

                    my name

remains in a crater
of its own making. Deep, with sides too tall,
my self would peer up at astonished faces
peeking over the edge to see who had dropped

onto this writer's page with such a force
that she is even afraid to spell.

Who is she saving from the weight of my name?

A current love, perhaps? One she stays with
like a pack of cigarettes she no longer smokes.
Still brand-loyal, but no longer craving.

Urban Spring

Winter wrings itself out. Noise sits at the surface
of an amplified water table and, after hibernation,
every stranger is suspect. A crush of people sit

at my shoulder, nose to my cheek, daring me
to acknowledge the woman in my alley: veins pop
in Pavlovian response to her lips on some cock.

We share an address, but I am a guest. My city cultivates
a new crop of feenin' thieves & kids fixing fights for livestream
footage, uploaded, earning stripes on urban uniforms.

Graffiti blooms like latent violence, revealing my city's leanings
toward hierarchy instead of living. New plumes of ego blossom
on the side of buildings: canvas for territories claimed.

Our neighborhood is pissed on, owned by whichever
pimp-hitch is nastiest. It's spring and I am someone's bitch.

Returning to Work in Tipp City, OH, After the Women's March

He tells me about his weekend
and how the wrestling arena was packed.
Some had signs—the usual, he says:
We the People, John Cena is still a tool!
My wife thinks I'm at Bible study.
That one was funny, he says.

There was music of course, not live,
but, you know, loud music and
everyone pumping their fists in the air
like it's a rock concert. The music
really telling the crowd what to feel.
You know who's coming to the ring
as soon as the first note hits.
It's easy to tell who the villain is.

Jericho choked Samoa Joe with an electric cable
and wrapped his body with barbed wire
and hit him with a chair to the chest
and his hands were tied behind his back
and he couldn't protect himself at all
and he slipped in his blood when he tried to stand
and you couldn't help but feel a part of something huge,

you know, when you're surrounded by thousands,
all chanting, *Yes! Yes! Yes!* and you want the finisher,
the one that really puts the wrestler out of his misery,
but you don't want it to end. Finishing moves are way
more tame now anyway. Chair shots to the head
are illegal now. So are curb stomps. You can't just crush
a man's skull with your boot anymore. Aw, no, no.
Don't worry—it's not real blood. It's all in good fun.
And the promoters already know who's going to win.

Bucha, Ukraine

—after *Schoolhouse #3 Bucha* by artist Lynn Cox

Let's agree, this war has nothing to do with children
so perhaps we'll start with the uninvited:

guests who peer at Bucha through a despot's kaleidoscope
of lies. Their tanks stalled outside the crown city
they'd rather seize, they use the citizens for sport.
        They defecate in the living room.
           They rape in the basement.

No, not here. It's too heavy. Let's be grateful for the sound of tanks
that shield us from the sound of what is crushed under them.

Here a woman in her garden warns her lilies. It is early March,
they have shown their heads too soon,
they will be cut short by forecasted frost
Do not mistake the sun for safety, she tells them
and, before she is shot, they whisper the same.

You're right, of course. A thin metaphor won't stop a war.

So let's start instead with sunflower seeds
and the grandma who orders a Russian soldier
to pocket them so that his corpse will bloom
brightly near her grandson's body.
        She offers them like a coffin spray.
          She offers them like a curse.

Brightness and seeds.

So, we can agree, this war has everything
to do with children.

All Together Now

The street-scrubbers from last night
are among the crowd, their hands still vibrating
with the feel of bristles on brick. Water pools
at the downslope of granite curbs though
Dayton has not seen rain in ten days.
The media tents camped on the sidewalk
force you into the crush of people
facing the vigil's stage. You move upstream.
Sometimes your shoulders are pulled
by the current opposing you. Because
in America you have the luxury of returning
to the closed street where nine people
were killed so early that morning you say *last night,*
because you still have the luxury of defiance,
the belief about lightning strikes and all that,
you are compelled to join hundreds to shout
at cardboard leaders from the capital city
who will cross the stage like two-dimensional
ducks. You will aim your grief at them
as scripted. Because the only thing different
about your city's trauma is the antique bricks
you stand on. Wax from vigil candles will seal
the names into stone. Candles doled out
from grocery bags. Candles already half-spent
from the tornadoes or KKK protest or
maybe this tragedy was so hot the candles
burned themselves in anticipation of politicians
invoking God, which is to say, it's out of their hands.
And the release of doves. Because this is America
and we are nothing if not symbolic.
But before the singing of Cohen's "Hallelujah"—
which is about violence and sex after all
and how fitting, America? —you will drape
yourself over a stranger because in passing him
you recognize your own ashes. And if you have

woven your bodies just right, both of his arms
under yours, you will let your knees soften.
If he pulls you closer, if you trust his ability
to hold your grief, if your cheek meets the soft part
of his chest, you will cry, open-mouthed,
stopping the flow of the crowd.

Witness

—Chautauqua Institution, August 12, 2022

Having been taken unaware,
my brain now expects

violence like weather,

changing but persistent.
My mind spools ahead
creating images

of horror. It predicts

crushed metal in this sea
of traffic, a car eating through
the yellow line, crumpled

steel glinting like
sun-caught ripples
on Chautauqua Lake

or like knives.

I am told that waiting
for a person to walk out
of that high-rise window,

as certain as I wait for an elevator,
are my thoughts protecting me.
I am not spared premonitions

of limbs swimming

through their own airy regret,
but, rather, the surprise of it.

My senses prepare me now
for the blood before
it happens so that

I do not delay this time,
do not take so long
recognizing the attempt on a life.

Forgive Us Our Trespasses

What are the words, the comforting
as we forgive those who trespass against us

words, rhythmic pulses sung or chanted
as we forgive those who trespass against us

that can rescue you or talk you
as we forgive those who trespass against us

into anything? What words are whispered
as we forgive those who trespass against us

until their meaning is rubbed smooth
as we forgive those who trespass against us

as seaglass. These are the words to which we return
as we forgive those who trespass against us.

IV

Hereditary Border

Forty years after an electrified threat kept them
                    from greener fields,
there remains a grazed line of grass

across which red deer do not pass.
                    In war times,
a hot wire fence kept their kind behind a barrier.

Now, fed on their mother's mother's memory of fear,
                    fawns learn
where safety lies. They track the path south to north,

holding a hereditary border. From above,
                    guard tower mice
imagine them licking steel briars from their fur.

Though free to roam, the deer maintain the pace
                    of captive men.
Hooves hard-pack ground the brown of worn leather.

They graze. They stop. Their skin flinches
                    with ghosts of volts.
They turn. They graze. They feed to the edge.

How Wonderful to Love

—after Dorthea Lasky

How wonderful to be in love
And to have children to love
And who love each other
Who love to call each other
And say *I love you* and do it
So lovingly every Sunday at least
You know I've always loved that sweater
That card you sent was lovely
And, damn, that review you wrote
For that movie we both loved
I loved it
And your TikTok? Love
My boss is so very lovable
I love how well this program works
What's not to love about this day
And all the lovely people in it
Walking and loving each other
Through this storm
Love the ice and how it rattles
The glass and your memories
Seeking a target to love
I love that
And that your dinner's already made
But you won't remember
Who I am to you
Lovely
Goodbye
Heading out
To start my leaving
Finally
Your past
Slowed to a lovely pace
Love

Final Exam

Of twenty-four students, she alone
is not bent over a desk—though no less
dutiful. The students repeat on paper
what I've taught them: characters persevere
or they do not.

Her belly no longer allowing her back
to curve, her legs spread to shelve
the warren of her womb. Induced tomorrow,
she takes this high school test—no wires or gel—
her last examination. Erect, she bubbles answers,
some correct,

and I wonder what I can teach this girl
whose body coaxes bones to relax,
intuits the need to loosen ligaments,
opens the cervical eye until all is revealed
and undulations guide fresh life through
a flooded canal.

Each month my own body flushes itself
of chance, my pelvic bones in permanent
stasis. *Bubble, instead, a pattern*, I want to say,
of your new baby's name—more potent, surely,
than this recycled test, stale from all the years
of being taken.

Body of Work

for not much longer I have eggs
inside me to spare offered
like fireworks to the dusk
uncalled for sparking nonetheless

smear them over your longing
and stop your need to pull them
from the sky by handsful
pocket as many as you can

into your own cervix
if that's where eggs belong
I never bothered to learn
knowing full well

they let my mother return
for her high school exams
they gave her a card table
to tuck her belly under

but no help
in back of the class
she would have me
and no other and her mother

threatened to throw herself
over Niagara Falls rather than
let a baby catch its breath
outside of her this is what

I came from the roar of
the river reminding me
I was not of maternal stock
it is right of course

when has water ever lied
it reflects only truth
flushes out the wanted
and unwanted alike

expelled upon the shore
to see what has capacity
to crawl forward from froth
and make new life

take these eggs
don't need them
never wanted them
I come from a long line
of not wanting

Language is the only homeland.

—Czesław Miłosz

Did I expect Poland to welcome me
into her fold? That I could translate
train announcements because I carry
memories of butter-shellacked pierogi

glistening on my plate next to golumpki
with cabbage leaves tucked tight
like hospital corners around beef and rice.
Instead, I wander village to village,

a common tourist eating ice cream
and asking for the bathroom
with my third-generation lexicon.
I make eye contact like an orphan

as if some *babcia*, tottering home
with market bag handles hewing
grooves in her hands, will recognize

the green in my eyes, divine, *Sylvie's girl!*,
pass me her burden, and show me home.
In her kitchen, she nestles beets,
each a solidified heart, into my hand.

We drink borscht from jelly jars,
chatter about the neighbor's cat
and the square's fountain—still dry.
When her husband returns from work,

he won't be surprised to see me
at the sink, feet bare on the braided rug,
tossing buttered noodles, waiting
for my attic room to air out.

St. Michael Taxiarchi's Shrine, Tarpon Springs, Florida

—for Grandma Sylvia

God knows I'm a non-believer,
but I slide my money into the painted box

and light a cream taper—two fingers
long, slender as lightning—in your name.

Because you would have,
I say the prayer of St. Michael,

archangel of battles, miracle worker.
I stare at his faith-tempered sword, but

it was your fierceness I prayed to.
His image, more tangible now than your own,

repeats on four walls like
a crowd of witnesses.

Going Home Again

There is a white-collar cost to remaining
true blue. Outsider status comes with a degree.
You can go home again but there is an overly polite

emphasis on plans to accommodate and I know
I haven't forgotten how to drive in the snow, but
I am offered the 4x4 like a guest, and my vinaigrette's

fancy which is to say *snobby*, and a bit *salty*, which is to say
salty—not surprising because I am Lot's wife, nameless
and a warning for those who think they are better: if you are

willing to leave the others behind to burn,
you don't deserve a return engagement.

Luxury of Snow

As if a blizzard can trigger muscle memory,
my cells slow through my own system
conserving themselves. Boots and a shovel

stand at the door like my mom had put them there
herself. I wait out the storm with a luxury
that my parents did not have. I sit surrounded

by fireworks of ice pulsing against each pane
remembering my mom leaning towards the windshield
as if these extra inches kept her from snow blindness.

As if her concentration alone ensured each tire's purchase
on slick roads. She willed the flakes from needling
their way into her vision and followed tail lights blinking

their own desperation. This train of cars slowed
enough to share a pledge to keep moving forward
for those behind and ahead. That each driver will go

where they have to be. That they will get paid, or fed,
or offer themselves for the same. I watch the snow
swirl itself, guilty of having nowhere I need to go.

Wherever You Go

I.

You hold hands with the fortune-teller
and ask in every language you know
if your parents are proud. She tells you
she foresees the future. Too late
for your question. Too late
to do anything about that now.

II.

The exercise is simple enough:
everyone starts on the same line,
and, if the privilege applies,
take one step forward or back
according to your zip code.

III.

You have forgotten names for most tools
your dad used and how they felt in your hand.
Downtown is sanitized by money.
There is nowhere you would not go anymore.
No man paying you to take his dog,
the collar at the end of the leash empty.
You read a map. You download the city's app.
Continue as guest.

IV.

How different is the mass shooting
in your hometown from the one
in your current city from the one
at your place of work from the one
from the one from the one from

V.

Wherever you go
there
you are.

Inverted Water

Each summer the water flipped itself: a great lake
turning skyward, warming its underbelly. Frigidity
found us, not when we least expected it, but when

we had forgotten to expect it at all. Temperature-
testing toe dips dispensed with, we dashed
toward the deep, lured by warmth we believed

would last our entire lives. We ignored the bite
below our treading feet though the cold
truth had passed through childhood lore,

no science but our skin to know the world
had gone upside-down. Somewhere along the way,
college perhaps, when learning occurs at the expense

of all else, I looked up this unlikely magic. It's true:
seasonal lake stratification. But who doesn't prefer
the fairytale over an expert-explained inversion,

wanting to hold the spell of not knowing
a bit longer? Now, states away from the lake
which spent decades heaving its dead at my feet,

I choose to believe the world can magically
right itself. Can bring the warmth
back to the surface where it belongs.

Notes

"Moving Up Day," Rebuttal," "Calculating Exposure," and "Rosie No More" were informed by research into Bethlehem Steel Corporation including information and direct quotes from Frank A. Behum Sr.'s *30 Years Under the Beam: Bethlehem Steel Exposed As told by those who worked there.*

The form of "Subpono" was inspired by Mohja Kahf's poem "Lowering of the Gaze."

"All Together Now" is a response to the mass shooting in my current city, Dayton, Ohio, on August 4, 2019. Though the gunman was fatally shot by officers less than 40 seconds after he began shooting, he had killed nine people in the entertainment district of the city.

On August 12, 2022, my wife and I were in attendance at the Chautauqua Institution for Salman Rushdie's conversation with Henry Reese about the need for safe havens for writers in exile. Prior to the discussion, an attacker ran on stage, stabbing Mr. Rushdie repeatedly before audience members and Chautauqua staff wrestled the assailant to the ground. "Witness" was written, partly, in response to this attack.

"Hereditary Border" came into being from the BBC article "Czech deer still avoid Iron Curtain" which details that groups of red deer between Czechoslovakia and Germany border do not cross the area where electrified fences formerly stood. The deer, which had been fitted with GPS tracking collars in 2014, would have been born *after* the fences had been removed.

The form of "How Wonderful to Love" was inspired by Dorthea Lasky's poem "Is It a Burden."

Appreciation

This manuscript was completed with the invaluable gift of time and funding from the Ohio Arts Council and the Fine Arts Work Center. Thank you to Craig Dicken and Debra Kaiser, the graphic-design team who visually represented, beyond my imagination, this collection of poems. To Hayley Mitchell Haugen at Sheila-Na-Gig Editions who welcomed my work into the conversation.

Thanks to the Greenville Poets—Cathryn Essinger, David Garrison, Janet E. Irvin, Suzanne Kelly-Garrison, Belinda Rismiller, and Myrna Stone—for their attention and care of my work. Gratitude also to Dr. Adrienne Cassel for recognizing my poet's heart long before I did. I miss her every time I pick up a pen.

Thank you Bill Barry and Frank Behum Sr., for research to which I turned time and again, and Judith Romanowski for sharing her childhood memories of Buffalo. And to countless steelworkers, named and unnamed, for their labor.

Heartfelt thanks to July Westhale, Amber Wong, and Erin Hill, whose own work I admire and whose generous friendship, support, and advice propel me still. To the instructors and colleagues in the Lesley University MFA Community, especially the Tuesday Group, who fed me in so many ways, and Sharon Bryan for her literal and metaphorical open door.

Thank you to my dad for his gift of writing and respect for words. And to my mom, my consummate supporter in all endeavors. Though she did not live to see this book in print, she willed it into being.

And to my wife Carrie. Her unflagging belief in the value of creative endeavors opened a level of fulfillment I never knew existed. I am so grateful for the life we've built together.

About the Author

Aimee Noel has twice been awarded the Ohio Art Council's Individual Excellence Award for poetry and was an OAC Fellow at the Fine Arts Works Center. Her poems are published in journals such as *Ecotone, Witness, Michigan Quarterly Review* and elsewhere. Transplanted from the shores of Lake Erie, she now lives with her wife in Dayton, Ohio. Find more at aimeenoel.net

Sheila-Na-Gig Editions